www.tredition.de

AF196325

Angwi Elizabeth Wanye

Entrepreneurship

An African Perspective

© 2016 Angwi Elizabeth Wanye

Verlag: tredition GmbH, Hamburg

ISBN
Paperback: 978-3-7345-5865-8
Hardcover: 978-3-7345-5866-5
e-Book: 978-3-7345-5867-2

Printed in Germany

Content

Preface

This book shows the compelling effort to mesh theory into practice. The information in this book compels you to re-examine your environment and take action. It describes how to tailor your knowledge and develop your society.

It is a practical guide for practitioners who provide counselling and planning services. It is also for pupils and students who want to develop their mind set. It is helpful for organizational development in different institutions. *Entrepreneurship: An African Perspective* is an easy to read book which demonstrates how you can transform your ideas into practice.

Acknowledgement

Special thanks go to all my colleagues and friends for their support and suggestions made on this topic. Special thanks go to Tabot Kingsley for his pictures. I appreciate your direct contribution on this field.

Special thanks also go to Abam Sydney, Wolfgang Azipon and Angel Blake for their alternative views and discussion on certain topics.

Not forgetting the special strength I got from my family to complete this project. Sarah Boehme, Fabian Boehme, Karl Boehme, Eva Boehme, Harald Boehme and Francisca Schutz-Glaeser. Thank you all for your support.

About the Editor

Rachelle Blake, PA, MHA, is a Global Senior Strategic Healthcare Information Technology Leader and Global HIT Workforce Subject Matter Expert. She is Founder, CEO and President of Omni Micro Systems, Inc. and Omni Micro Solutions, Inc., in the United States, and CEO, Founder and Managing Director of Omni Micro Systems & Omni Med Solutions UG (mini-GmbH) in Germany, an international family of full-scale health information consulting and technology development companies in operation for nearly a decade on a global level.

She has authored four books, including three textbooks, and a variety of instructional manuals, curricula, computer-based training modules, presentations and white papers.

Introduction

When people have the capacity and willingness to develop, organize and manage a business venture along with any of its risks in order to make a profit, we talk about **entrepreneurship**. However, Entrepreneurship does not only end there, according to Maria Minniti, a leading author on entrepreneurship and economic growth and professor at Babson College. It has a broader description. She said Entrepreneurship is more of an awareness of individuals to make changes that will improve their lifestyle. It does not necessarily mean starting a new business but also solving a problem or choosing to change a direction in order to save time. Entrepreneurship is as an attribute to human behaviour. This book focuses on Entrepreneurship from an economic perspective by being innovative and starting a new business. The practice of entrepreneurship is not only building a business that is competitive on the local market but also analysing the possibility of a business in Africa in order to interact on the global market. This material incorporates the role of education in business building as well as focuses on how to acquire funding and write down a good business plan.

The fast growing population in Africa, with significant growth of the working population, shows that Africa needs entrepreneurs with new and innovative ideas to match this growing work force. There is sufficient land, labour and natural resources which, when used effectively, will yield profit and promote growth in many African nations. The citizens should grasp the Entrepreneurial spirit and innovate, take risks and compete on the global market. In many areas of Africa, there is lack of basic knowledge and technology that promotes growth. This does not make **innovation** impossible; it shows that there is still a lot to accomplish. The citizens have to be aware of their environment, build up a mind-set that is innovative and try to develop their immediate environment. This book portrays African economic growth in the 21st century and encourages their citizens to be entrepreneurs. Education should be in a way that encourages children right from kindergarten to be aware of their environment and think of ways to improve it. This book explains the development going on in some African countries as well as provides some guidelines on how to get started as an entrepreneur. There are many projects going on in Africa which are interesting for **investors**, for example the 650-kilometer railway built to link up the Ethiopian capital of Addis Ababa and the Port of Doraleh in Djibouti. The grand Ethiopian renaissance dam and the plan to build the Konza Techno City in over 5,000 acres of land, 64km south of Nairobi. Investors usually shy away from supporting African investments because of high risk and little profit. However, investing in the right project can result in significant return on investment.

The first chapter of this book focuses on education, including what education is and how to educate the children to be thinkers of tomorrow. Chapter Two discusses the role of Entrepreneurship in the African community, including what advantages it brings to the community and its growing population. Chapter Three focuses on African Growth. The Gross Domestic Product (GDP) will be analysed and discussed, why it grows in most African countries at such a rapid rate. Chapter Four shows the perspective of Entrepreneurship in Africa and the benefits and gains it brings to society. In Chapter Five, the vital role that women play in business management will be discussed. Women generally have far less capital than men and are very concerned about their families, but their role in business is important. For these reasons, it is important to know the role gender plays in Entrepreneurship and how it influences economic growth. Chapter Six analyses the influence of governmental rule on economic growth; meanwhile, Chapter Seven discusses the effects of corruption on start-ups. After taking a close look at the environment of an entrepreneur, this booklet goes further to explain how to get started with your business, including where and how to raise funds and write down a good business plan.

Creative Thinking

1. Describe an Entrepreneur.

2. Are there any entrepreneurial projects currently going on in your town?

3. How would you classify the projects?

Education

For many centuries, experience has shown that education is the key to success. Does **education** mean that we have to study up to the university level to be educated? Is being a professor, having a post-secondary degree, or simply completing a primary or secondary school education sufficient to be known as educated? Actually, education can be as simple as learning enough to face the challenges of life. What is enough in this case? And how can we weigh or classify it? The fact is, there is no complete learning. As time changes, new development and processes influence our ways of thinking, learning and the way we do things. So it is quite obvious that a person in a developing country like Cameroon or Kenya learns differently from those in the developed world.

Returning to traditional education, going to school is necessary. In Africa there is a need for more and well-equipped schools with good teachers. Everybody is talented in a specific way and in different fields of work. Education will help to build up your talent. This actually means that schools should focus on building children to be able to discover their talent. They should be educated to be responsible for themselves, build good relationships in life and support the society in which they live in through hard work. It does not necessary mean that the school has to be expensive or have the best buildings in town. But the context and content being taught is very important. The schools should adjust their teaching plan to make the children take responsibility of themselves. The Africans should teach children right from primary school to be aware of their environment and should consider how to improve it.

Taking steps toward improving society are taking step towards entrepreneurship. If schools succeed in making pupils curious about their environment, they will grow up with this drive and try to improve their lives. Education should teach children how profits are made. By doing so, aspects like **production, cash flow, marketing** and **leadership** will be learned in school.

The advantages and disadvantages of **capitalism** and how it works should be taught. The dictionary defines Capitalism as an economic system in which investment in and ownership of the means of production, distribution, and exchange of wealth is made and maintained chiefly by private individuals or corporations. Capitalism can also be seen as a social system that recognises individual rights. The government is actually there to defend these rights. Economically, this system promotes production and the free market, but on the other side, there is a growth of greed.

Another very important aspect of education is knowing about ourselves. We have to start learning from the primary level about ourselves. Teachers are there to accompany the children to know how complex human beings are. They should know their identity, challenges, denial, acceptance and struggle of everyday life. Through this they will be able to react appropriately in times of difficulties, fear, tension and happiness. They will be able to build relationships that truly suit them and choose the right professions for themselves. By doing so, education is a process meant for all.

Schools currently spend a lot of time teaching about ancient history and focusing on issues which are very abstract for African students. It is good to have a general knowledge about the issues around us, but the focus should be on our environment and how we can develop it. Children are normally very creative, curious and very willing to learn something new. If a child's curiosity is supported, he has the ability to think wider. If it is blocked or the child is prevented from having a say or asking questions about the things going on around him or her, then that child will not see the need to develop something and will be unable to apply what they have learnt positively on our society. They will actually be waiting for the government to provide them with jobs when they are done with their schooling.

<u>Creative Thinking</u>

1. How would you describe the educational system in your country?

2. What do you like or dislike about the system?

3. What are some things you might do differently to positively change the educational system?

The Role of Entrepreneurship

It is a challenge to recognize opportunities and have the willingness to take action even when under very difficult circumstances. If someone can shape his or her perspective in order to realize an idea, they have discovered the gateway to entrepreneurship. The willingness to act, as well as the amount of knowledge and information one has on a specific topic, is very important. The **information could be imperfect**, but that should not dissuade you from continuing. On the other hand, you may be armed with **perfect or asymmetrical information** based on an idea. Having a bright idea and the willingness to achieve something pushes an entrepreneur to look for more information about the topic. The amount of information one has also determines the amount of risk in place. The depth and clarity of the information determine the eventual outcome of your business.

However, Entrepreneurship can also evolve through uncertainty. Trying to find the unknown drives the Entrepreneur to search and discover new theories. The unknown involves risks. The success of an Entrepreneurs is determined not only in taking these risks, however, but in achieving something to make a profit. Profit is placed at the forefront, and in addition to many other things, it is always one of the main goals of running a business. Economists differentiate two models in this case, the bottom-up model and the top-down model. The **Bottom-Up Model** occurs when an Entrepreneur has an idea and realizes this idea with all the details in it into a business unit. The **Top-Down Model**, conversely, focuses on a problem and the solution to this problem. The Entrepreneur already has a picture in mind on how the end result is supposed to look like. He then breaks down his strategy to achieve his goals. In the end, it does not really matter if you start at the top or at the bottom; what you will need to do is to challenge yourself to move out of your comfort zone and make sure that the whole business idea is complete.

The behaviour of an Entrepreneur could also be seen from two different perspectives: the **micro** and the **macro** level. At the micro level, entrepreneurs come out with an idea and work towards it. Through this they improve or change their present state. It is a bottom up movement. At the macro level, the entrepreneur looks for the solution of a certain problem. This could be, for example, a search for a solution of water shortage in a certain region; a top-bottom analysis.

Critically looking at the situation in Africa at the moment, there are a lot of small businesses owned by the poor and middle class. These businesses are mainly based on their daily needs and the direct needs of the citizens. This actually means that their businesses are on foodstuff and household needs, which are really not competitive on the global market. Some of these small businesses hardly have the capital to grow. It is more of a Hand-to-Mouth process. If these small businesses have the opportunity to get some support from the government or other organizations for instance small credit to support them, it will be of great use.

The focus on industrial and machinery products is still very low. A shift to this direction is of great significance. Bringing up an idea and getting support from the government or other financial institution is very important. Just having a good idea is not all that is needed to be an Entrepreneur, but taking action to accomplish the idea and getting support are also important requirements. If successful as an Entrepreneur, you may end up building something that creates jobs for the future generations.

Entrepreneurial Self-Assessment

Instructions: Read the following statements and questions, and answer with a "Yes" or "No" response to determine if you have the "Entrepreneurial Spirit"! If you answer "No" to any question or statement, this may be an area where you will find this booklet helpful to learn more and increase your potential to succeed as an Entrepreneur. There may be other questions that you can ask yourself that are not listed here, but this is a start to get you thinking...

Yes No

1. ☐ ☐ When I am at my job, I always want to do more than I am asked, or to go one step further.

2. ☐ ☐ I have great passion about my work, and in fact, sometimes I feel that I would do my favourite tasks even if I weren't being paid (but I am glad that I am).

3. ☐ ☐ When there is something new I am presented with at work, I always have a great idea about how to accomplish it.

4. ☐ ☐ Do you often like to look for solutions to problems?

5. ☐ ☐ Do people tell you that you like to think "outside the box"?

6. ☐ ☐ When I am put in a leadership position, I feel that I am up to the challenge.

7. ☐ ☐ I feel that I am self-motivated and that I do not usually need a lot of direction or supervision with my work activities.

8. ☐ ☐ I react to criticism in a constructive way, and can take feedback and apply it to my future endeavours.

9. ☐ ☐ Do you know of others who share your ideas, and with whom you could potentially build up a team who could support your ideas?

10. ☐ ☐ I can accept failures, and I can learn from them instead of being shut down by them.

African Economic Growth

According to *Africa Economic Outlook*, the **Real Gross Domestic Product (GDP)** growth of Africa in 2015 was approximately 5%. Some states in Africa have a growth rate higher than 7%. Before getting further into the details, let's explain what GDP actually means and how it comes to be. GDP represents the total value of goods and services a country produces over a period of time, typically a fiscal year. This is mostly done as compares to the previous year. That means if the GDP is 5%, the economy has grown 5%. This can be calculated either by adding up the total income everyone earned in a year (**Income approach**), by adding up the amount of money spent (**Expenditure approach**), or by summing up the amount of goods and services sold (**Output approach**). That means Gross Domestic Product (GDP) is:

Consumer spending (C)

+ Government Spending (G)

+ Business Capital Spending or Investment (I)

+ Net Export: Export-Import (NX)

C + G + I + NX = GDP

The most common approach is the expenditure approach and it is calculated by adding up the total Consumption, Government Spending, Investment and Net Export. Other factors like environmental harm or the value of the exportation of natural resources are not included. The GDP is used as a value to show the health of a country's economy. If a country is doing well, the GDP rises, the unemployment rate sinks, the employment rises, and with the increase in demand due to growth, wages also increase. A negative GDP growth is one of the determinants that indicate that a country is in or moving toward a recession.

According to Fig. 1, the highest GDP growth between 2013 and 2015 was seen in North African countries. There was a difference of about 2,2% growth from 2014 to 2015. Southern Africa was growing at a rate of about 4,2% next to East Africa, which experienced a slight growth from 2013 to 2015. On the other hand, there was a slight decrease in economic growth in West and central Africa from 2014 to 2015. All of this notwithstanding, west Africa has been the fastest growing region in Africa due to the boom in the oil market in Nigeria, for example. All in all, there is still high GDP growth in these areas as compared to the rest of the world.

Fig. 1

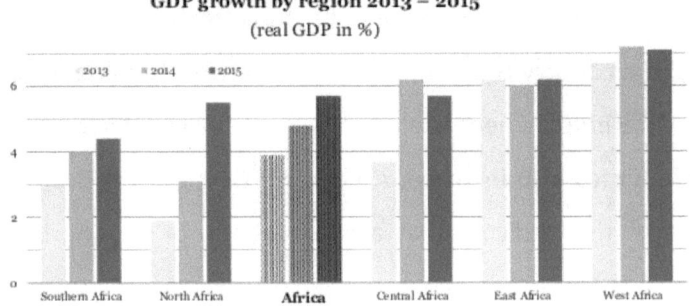

GDP growth projected to continue strongly in 2015. West Africa is the fastest growing region with growth projected at 7.1%.

Source: AfDB, OECD, UNDP, African Economic Outlook 2014

Source: AFDB, OECD, UNDP, African economic Outlook 2014[i]

After getting to know the meaning of GDP, Fig. 2 shows the real GDP growth of the 10 largest sub-Saharan economies in 2015. The real gross domestic product is inflation-adjusted. It is a measure that reflects the value of all goods and services produced in a given year, expressed in base-year prices. It is often referred to as "constant-price" or "inflation-corrected" GDP. Real GDP account for changes in the price level, and provides a more accurate figure, unlike **nominal**

GDP. The main difference between nominal and real values is that real values are adjusted for inflation, while nominal values are not. As a result, nominal GDP will often appear higher than real GDP.

Fig.2

REAL GDP GROWTH IN THE 10 LARGEST SUB-SAHARAN ECONOMIES IN 2015

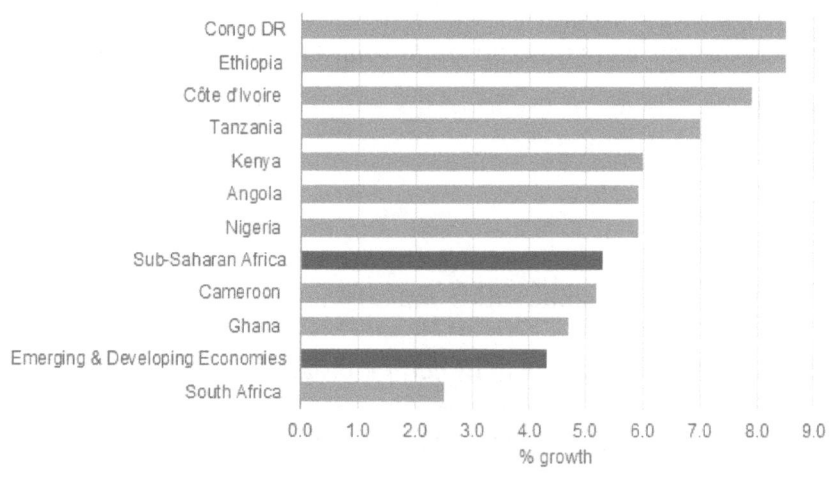

Source: Euromonitor International from national statistics/Eurostat/OECD/UN/IMF[ii]

Why is there such a high economic growth in Africa? Most African states solely depend on agriculture and other natural resources in international trade. They trade with less industrialized products. The **Africa Growth and Opportunity Act (AGOA)** and policy reforms in Africa have actually made some countries, like Lesotho and Uganda, increase their textiles exports. They are one of the beneficiaries of Agoa that provides for duty-free treatment for about 6,500 goods from eligible sub-Saharan African countries imported into the US market. Other countries have diversified into higher value agricultural products, which increases job opportunities and income earned by these states. The major Export of the above-mentioned states can be seen in Fig. 3

Fig.3 Major Export commodities and originating countries[iii]

Countries	Major Export commodities
Congo DM	Diamonds, gold, copper, cobalt, wood products, crude oil, coffee
Ethiopia	Coffee, gold, leather products, live animals, oilseeds
Cote D'Ivoire	Cocoa, coffee, timber, petroleum, cotton, bananas,

	pineapples, palm oil, fish
Tanzania	Gold, coffee, cashew nuts, manufactures, cotton
Kenya	Tea, horticultural products, coffee, petroleum products, fish, cement
Angola	Crude oil, diamonds, refined petroleum products, coffee, sisal, fish and fish products, timber, cotton
Nigeria	Petroleum and petroleum products 95%, cocoa, rubber
Cameroon	Crude oil and petroleum products, lumber, cocoa beans, aluminium, coffee, cotton
Ghana	Gold, cocoa, timber, tuna, bauxite, aluminium, manganese ore, diamonds, horticulture
South Africa	Gold, diamonds, platinum, other metals and minerals, machinery and equipment

According to Fig. 3, only South Africa exports machinery and equipment. International trade in the other countries is based on Agra products and natural resources.

The high GDP growth in Africa leads to an increase in per capita national income. An increase in income with little or no changes in the price of goods leads to a higher demand for goods and services. The increase in demand with low inflation shows that the states are economically stable. This creates a good environment for investment and partnership as well as entrepreneurship.

On the other hand, the gap between the rich and the poor is becoming wider. The positive effect of growth is focused on the rich, and the poor recognise very little from the country's growth. This issue is actually linked to the fact that most African countries export natural resources and Agra products. This sector creates little job opportunities for the citizen. The profits made remain at the managerial levels of the company. The workers gain very little from them. Meanwhile, companies that do not deal with exporting goods have no link to the profits and therefore realize less change in growth. That is why there is a high necessity for good governance, so that regulations can be made that benefit the nation as a whole, not specific companies or branches.

Africans import a lot of products out of Africa but then they have to trade among themselves. They import poverty, since what they bring into the country through purchasing ends up competing with commodities that are produced locally. They export jobs because they export raw materials instead of developing a product with higher value to export. Entrepreneurs should use this great opportunity with an enormous supply of raw materials and develop something new and useful for their own market. There are a lot of opportunities in Africa, but very few entrepreneurs. Africa needs entrepreneurs and these should not come from the outside, but should develop from within Africa itself. The government should let investors invest and build factories in Africa. Actually, exporting raw materials allows foreign nations to produce goods and then sell them back to the African states at almost 10 times the price.

There is a need to change the mind-set to one of strength and intelligence, realizing and accepting our environment the way it is, but building it up and telling our own stories instead of waiting on foreign aid and intervention. The Africans do not need to go out to look for jobs, but need to try to be more creative. Building up one's own business is creating security. It is security in the sense that the living standards of the citizens will improve and the young generation will not see the need to migrate out of their states.

<u>Creative Thinking</u>

1. How can we keep our environment clean?
2. What are the ways of processing garbage?
3. How do you cooperate with a partner to increase your profit to 10% in the garbage business?

From the Start-Up Perspective

After analysing economic growth in Africa, citizens will have the capacity to realize their potential and make progress. Progress comes along by acting independently and by being able to support oneself. It is a matter of dignity and self-reliance. Creating an opportunity for others to achieve something is the beginning of the end of aid. Aid in food and clothing will only help in the short run, but investment in businesses, education, healthcare etc., will enable citizens to have jobs that enable them to feed and educate their children. It is a matter of perspective. A desperate man, who is at all times trying to make ends meet, barely has time to think about the future and develop a process. His focus is to satisfy his basic needs, and therefore it is very important to create jobs to satisfy those needs. The goal should not be about waiting for someone to provide jobs, but for Africans to get started and be entrepreneurs. Africans do not have to wait for their government, or for foreign aid or for the willingness to travel out of the country, but must shift their mind-set to creativity. With some analysis, strategies, and openness to take risks and try something new, Africans can change their lives and the lives of others. As it is said, success is mostly within your reach; you just need to grab opportunities and use them wisely.

Humanitarian assistance and development investment are two sides of the same coin. Humanitarian assistance, in the form of foreign aid, is good to prevent death and very chronic suffering in rural areas. The **Official Development Assistance** (ODA) is aimed at ending extreme poverty by 2030 and leaves no one behind. ODA targets poverty reduction in developing countries, making and mobilising investment across the economic, social and environmental dimensions of sustainable development, to benefit the poorest people. It is rather unfortunate that ODA is allocated to countries with fewer people living in poverty and with lower depth of poverty. ODA also focuses on countries affected by conflict and fragility but still not all the states under these circumstances are prioritised in ODA allocation. Additionally, current allocations do not meet the need for sustained long-term financing to address the numerous overlapping and complex challenges faced by such states.

Although ODA is directly linked to development, foreign investment is not well managed to promote development. The largest investment in Africa comes from a few African countries like Nigeria and South Africa. But we expect more to come from the rest of the continent. Each job means a lot for the people, since it pulls the citizens out of poverty. There are numerous platforms and organisations that support businesses to grow. Entrepreneurs should use these opportunities and create something for themselves and the nation.

Having a role to play in African development, the other side of the coin is proving success and promoting it. The world's reaction on investment influences the growth of Africa as well. Foreign aid does not really empower the recipients, but foreign investment in countries in Africa does, yielding more fruits in aiding businesses to grow. It is rather unfortunate that Africa is trapped in unequal growth. Growth is elevated when the disparity among citizens is not very great. Although there is high growth in Africa at the moment, there is still a need for good infrastructure, education, healthcare system and good governance. Entrepreneurship changes the world through small and simple services. So those Africans who can make a move should go ahead and create relationships and joint ventures in their countries. Since 2015, there has been more support given to entrepreneurs in Africa. Not just capital is provided to them, but also good and quality training on how to go forward with their idea.

<u>Creative Thinking</u>

1. How does rejuvenation affect people's lives?
2. How does the Official Development Assistance (ODA) work in Africa?

Gender and Entrepreneurship

African women are very supportive. They support their families and make sure that the basic needs of the family are met. But then, they still play a very minor role in African society. Due to lack of sufficient capital, African women usually focus on small-scale businesses that meet their basic needs and those of their immediate family. Their businesses are mostly based on agricultural products and finished products which have a direct connection to their daily needs. Very few women have the possibility to stand up on their own and create businesses on long-term bases that can compete on the national and international market.

Worldwide, there are less women going into entrepreneurship than men. But this sequencing is gradually changing. More women are taking the chance of being financially stable and creating businesses for themselves. In Europe and the United States, there are many businesses owned by women. This is unlike Africa, where there are only a handful of women business owners, who can compete nationwide. This is because of the status of the women. The men still play the leading role in African society and the women continue to subordinate and have the role of a housewife, bearing children and taking care of the household. They hardly have enough capital to stand up on their own, and even those who do want to be independent are supressed by their husbands or their environment. Of course, there are exceptions to this, as there are also African men who love and support strong women. Some of them even push their women to be independent and propel them forward. These men provide good examples by promoting equality, as they realize that women have a major role to play in their society rather than just being household help. It is due to reasons such as this that in most African countries, initiatives are being taken to create awareness and encouragement to African women who want to be entrepreneurs. Although these initiatives do exist, however, there are very few of them and women rarely take advantage of them. Society has a responsibility to encourage women to realize that these opportunities exist and that they need to use them.

There are many institutions and banks like the United Bank of Africa (UBA) that helps to provide long-term support for women and men who are entrepreneurs. They provide long-term low-rate capital, which enables a sustainable eradication of poverty. Although entrepreneurship focuses on the individual trying to build up a successful business, women should get together with the aim of business cooperation in order to enhance their income potential. In rural society and in some states, women meet on a monthly basis to contribute money and support themselves. Venues like these could be used to innovate something new. If two or more women put their heads together and try to create something, they will probably be more successful than standing alone. The information flow through teamwork helps strengthen businesses and promote growth.

Successful start-up ideas that have grown into good and stable businesses should be mentors for upcoming entrepreneurs. As stated previously, the risk of an entrepreneur depends on the information he or she has about the innovation and how to turn the idea into a successful business. The information flow and how to acquire this information greatly depends on the level of education and the environment we live in. The use of IT has actually widened the information flow worldwide, but there are still many areas that do not have Internet and therefore do not have access to such information. Other regions may have Internet coverage, but they do not know how to effectively use it.

The need for citizens to be entrepreneurs and try to build something for themselves should be taught in schools. This mind set should be developed at a very early stage, so it can influence their way of thinking. In some areas in Africa, parents still prefer to send their male children to school and the female children are left home. This practice is mostly seen in the remote areas of Africa and these communities need to be enlightened on the advantages of getting their daughters educated, for every child has the right of education.

Entrepreneurs mostly get their inspiration from their environment and then think beyond. The environment influences a person's way of thinking and behaviour. If your daily activity is to go to the farm, clean the house, and take care of cattle, then you have to think about how to achieve these daily chores using less time. Think about what you can do to make things better for you, how you can cook using less firewood and still have your meal ready on time, how to make better and stronger brooms to sweep the compound, what to do to improve your harvest on the same piece of land etc. Women do most of the above-mentioned activities, only they get less profit from them.

All in all, most women have no capital, or less than their male counterparts, to start a competitive business. Their businesses are mostly based on Agra products. Most of the industrial products are imported from overseas. But still, many African countries are striving to diversify their income and promote women. They strive on creating numerous opportunities for trade and investment in order to attract foreign investors.

Creative Thinking

1. How can a female entrepreneur improve on your market and farm yields by 15%?
2. What are the things you could do to empower women in your society?
3. How would you enlighten parents to educate their daughters?

The Influence of Governmental Rule

Political stability has a very important role to play in African development and growth. There have been some improvements in the political rule in Africa. This can be seen in the last presidential elections in some states, where there have been fair presidential elections and there is a willingness to change. Leaders are now trying to compete with each other and trying to bring out the best they can. Through this, the political situation in some states is becoming more stable and government policy is becoming more predictable.

The willingness of Africans in the diaspora to invest back home is increasing. There is a need to interact with each other both economically and politically, creating an atmosphere of economic growth. There should be a system to support entrepreneurs, since they will need capital to invest. Political leaders should take responsibility to create a political environment for businesses to succeed. Government should provide good infrastructure, including roads, education, healthcare, etc. The private sector also has an important role to play, and should not just wait for the government to react. Innovation, hard work, and personal and collective market initiative will change the state and governmental decisions. The commitment to succeed is all about value and the vision necessary to drive sustainable growth around Africa.

Instead of political leaders following selfish ambitions that only lead to personal desire and benefits for their immediate family, they should rethink leadership and consider what true leaders ought to do. They should build up institutions and support entrepreneurs. There are several ways to support start-ups. For example, leaders can:

> ➤ Create a basis for development by building up a good infra-structure and good roads
> ➤ Rethink foreign aid; they should not only concentrate on saving lives, but should also focus on empowering the people.
> ➤ Promote investment by creating an environment that promotes development
> ➤ Build an educational system that teaches the skills of good leadership, entrepreneurship, relationship building and self-esteem.
> ➤ Empower women and promote female education.

Growth goes along with capitalism. Development causes a gradual shift from agriculture to technology. The government should support new technology and investment since it creates new jobs, promotes growth and eradicates poverty. However, the government still needs to promote agriculture, since it is the key to survival.

Government should maximise development instead of simply spending time writing programmes on how to distribute foreign aid. Frequently a lot of time is invested in allocating the budget provided in different sectors as aid instead of showing more concern toward the private sector. Although there is a lot of aid coming into Africa, remittance compared to direct investment is still uneven. There will be a greater expansion in growth by supporting the private sector and entrepreneurs. The private sector has to know how to manage its own capital and build a great network. In this case, capitalism is supporting a specific sector that supports long-term investment. **Inclusion (inclusive capitalism)** is a very important component of this. Inclusion is when every citizen receives the value and outcome of growth. There should be the ability to touch as many lives as possible, giving value to each and every one's life.

Free market possibility for investors in Africa could create more jobs and promote growth. This is only possible if the investment is not in total control by foreigners. The government should go into diplomatic agreements that favour both parties. With such agreements investors will be unable to impose their terms and conditions on the state. For example, the relationship between China and most African countries was based on the Non-Intervention Act. Notwithstanding the fact that China is more interested in Africa's raw materials, they also build infrastructure in exchange. Although there are other aspects like human rights, which will not be discussed here, the fact is, China does not intervene in the country's politics. They are not there to build companies for the Africans. The Africans should do it themselves.

Moreover, growth should not favour the rich against the poor. Structural adjustment should promote farmers, for example. If the government subsidises the production of rice in his country, the farmer gets the incentive to produce more rice, and less rice will be imported into the country. We need to get rid of barriers within Africa and promote trade among ourselves. When the barriers are open, there will be more economic flow. According to African Economic Outlook, trade between African nations is only 11%; therefore Africans should promote free trade between them and heighten investment.

The African population is growing in a very fast rate. Statistics show that by 2050, the strongest workforce will be in Africa. According to the United Nations' Department of Economics and Social Affairs, the population of Africa will increase by 25% (Fig. 4). The working age population, citizens between 15-64 years old, will be in Africa. This is a great advantage for the government to start planning to provide jobs for its workers and prevent them from migrating out of their countries. But if the governments do not do anything to promote growth in their countries, they are going to lose the workforce to the outside world. Presently, more people acquire wealth since the economy is growing, but if the government does not create possibilities for these workers to stay, they will migrate. The government should do long-term planning on how to support entrepreneurs and promote investment.

Fig. 4 Regional distribution of global population by region, 2010 and 2050 (2013)[iv]

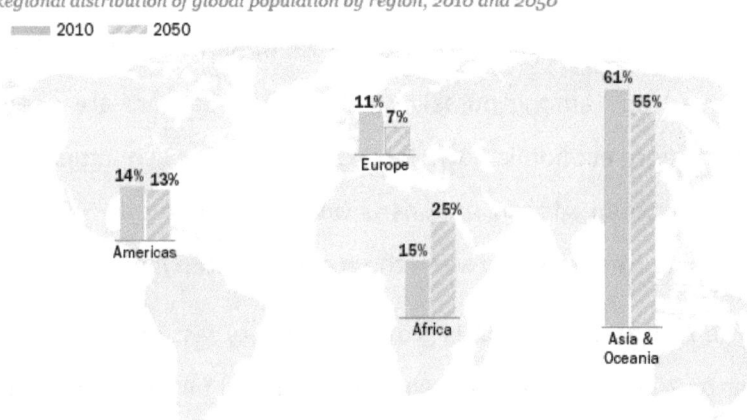

Regional distribution of global population by region, 2010 and 2050

2010   2050

14% 13% Americas

11% 7% Europe

25% 15% Africa

61% 55% Asia & Oceania

Source: United Nations, Department of Economic and Social Affairs, *World Population Prospects: 2012 Revision*, June 2013, http://esa.un.org/unpd/wpp/index.htm

PEW RESEARCH CENTER

An effective taxation system is necessary in every state. The government should create a taxation system that will provide income to support the nation. Drawing up a good and reasonable agenda for the state on how to handle taxes is very necessary. This includes setting a tax rate that will not be a burden on the citizen and at the same time will yield revenue for the state. Economic models should be based on the situation in Africa. It will not be fruitful to apply the models used in the developed world on a 1:1 ratio. The taxation system should be adjusted to meet the needs and standards of the African states. If these standards are taken into consideration, then a good agenda on taxation will further economic growth and reduce poverty.

<u>Creative Thinking</u>

1. How does an effective taxation system function?
2. How does an inclusive governmental system work?

Corruption and other obstacles for Start-Ups

Africa is full of opportunities. A shift from trading with raw materials to manufacturing and building new companies is a challenging step to take for Africans. However, these challenges make the country self-sufficient by using their own raw materials to create more economic activities for the continent.

There are some limitations for manufacturing in emerging markets in Africa. The economic system in many African countries is still **corrupt** and one country is out to dupe another. This only retards growth instead of promoting it. The biggest problem with growth in Africa is non-inclusive growth. Income is not equally shared. Very few people have a lot of income, but the majority do not. What they do is provide help to the poor. This is actually a kind gesture but it is not progressive. Most of the very poor are less educated and therefore it is not easy to get jobs in new companies needing skilled labour. There-fore it is very necessary to invest in agriculture, where unskilled work-ers could be employed and be encouraged to improve their situation.

Corruption is a problem in many African nations, but this does not stop business from evolving. Corruption is everywhere, but at dif-ferent levels and in different forms. In many parts of the world, in order to work in a company, you have to place an application for the job. If your application best suits the job profile, you will get the job. There are also cases where getting the job is due to connections. It does not depend on what you know but who you know. In Africa, not only the connection matters, but in some cases you pay to get a job or to support your business. This makes it difficult for entrepreneurs to start flourishing. There are initiatives set up in many countries to tackle corruption. The initiatives are not effective enough in most African countries but this should not be a hindrance to entrepreneurship. A good businessman understands his business and will always strive to follow it no matter what. It is of course necessary to know your environment and to come up with strategies that best suit your business and avoid corruption as much as possible.

Security is also a very critical issue in Africa. When there is a lot of theft and political instability, a business has difficulty growing. A strong security system is very important. The police should be active in finding criminals rather than taking bribes on the streets. There are a lot of terror forces, which diminish investment. Terror attacks and tribal clashes equate to assaults on the economy. This can only diminish by tackling economic inclusion. This can prevent people with less income and education from feeling ignored or joining terrorist forces in order to be heard.

Trust between African states should be stronger, and the states should strengthen trade amongst themselves. Stereotypes basically focus on the negative aspects in Africa and this does not show the face of Africa as a whole. Africa is portrayed as politically demoralized and torn apart by war. But how many people suffer as a result of this? Conversely, what are the opportunities for change that this presents? Foreign investment brings about new skills, technology, training, new ideas, etc. These aspects increase competition. The focus should be on the positive aspects and the development of the continent. Investment policies should suit the private sector and not only foreign investors. Domestically, citizens have to be involved in all investment plans.

After this analysis of the economic situation in Africa, you will next learn how to get started as an entrepreneur, including what you need to get started and where to find support for your project. Note that this is just a guideline to help you accomplish your goals. Entrepreneurs evolve in many ways and these attributes are there to help and direct you to find your way forward.

<u>Creative Thinking</u>

1. What are the possible ways to fight corruption?
2. What would you do if you were confronted with an act of corruption?
3. What are some methods you could use to ensure a corrupt-free Start-Up?

How to get started

Using Africa's local commodities to create jobs is taking a step forward. It is the beginning of transformation and this transformation is seriously needed in Africa. To invent Inventing something new means creating a new commodity that does not have a value at that moment. If this invention is commercialized, it generates a value and we call it an **innovation**. Entrepreneurs with brilliant ideas who can innovate something are needed in Africa. More than one third of the African population owns a cell phone, but there is nearly no production of cell phones on the African continent. They are mostly imported goods, although some of the raw materials used in producing these phones are from Africa.

There are of course many ways to get started as an entrepreneur. Here are some hints as to how an entrepreneur evolves.

➢ **Technology push**: If the necessary technology is at hand, you try to innovate something based on the possibilities you have and then you look for a means to market your new creation.

➢ **Market pool**: In this case, you look at what is lacking in the market and what is being needed most that will make a profit. With the interest of increasing your profit, there is a push to innovate and do something new.

➢ **Passion to be an entrepreneur**: To be passionate about what you do means you really enjoy what you do and therefore put forward a lot of effort to make it work. A real entrepreneur is passionate about his or her work and will do everything to overcome obstacles that get in the way.

Passion for your business is a very important aspect in starting a business but do not let passion override the marketing idea and the technology you possess. Having passion for your business makes you excited and committed. At times it is not so easy to determine what you are passionate about. You have to try different jobs to determine what you actually love to do most. If it is something you love to do, then you will always be energized and will not feel tired or bored when doing it. Do your best and never let an excuse hold you back. Strive to do your best in what you are doing without having regrets.

There are strong family ties within African communities, which you can use in a positive way. Remember to stay focused and to follow your ambition. If you think helping those around you will keep you focus and motivated, do that. Your empathy towards them will help them to support you, and this in turn gives you the opportunity to build a strong team. But remember, your success is not based on your empathy or kind-heartedness but on your ambition and passion for what you do.

Basic skills needed

Basic management skills are something you need in order to get started. Entrepreneurs should be able to determine if they have the right resources for their innovation even if there are others working with them. Change is at times necessary, but an entrepreneur uses change wisely. An entrepreneur strives to be the best in the world. In this case, an entrepreneur must know how to calculate risks and when to take them.

The ability to develop a vision for your company or a particular idea and to inspire employees to pursue the vision and be successful in it is known as effective leadership. This skill permits you to do whatever it takes to achieve your goal, starting from anywhere along the journey. When an entrepreneur fails, loses or feels weak and depressive, he or she stands up again and takes on new challenges. The entrepreneur thinks about the next right step to take. Everyone makes mistakes, but we must learn from them.

The third skill you will need is the ability to plan and be committed. Entrepreneurs must be able to develop **business plans** to meet goals in a variety of areas, like construction, sales, finance, marketing and production. Because of the ever-present lack of time and cash flow, you will need to be well disciplined in your engagements.

Entrepreneurs also need communication skills. Entrepreneurs should be able to explain, discuss, sell and market their goods or services. Recognize self-worth and believe in yourself. Do not let others talk you down. **Visualize** exactly what you want and have self-esteem. Honour yourself and you will be able to break through, helping both yourself and others.

Being able to market your innovation is also necessary for entrepreneurial success. Marketing skills enable you to run the race as hard as you can. Your business is about you and you have to dedicate full energy to what you do. You should not focus on those behind or around you trying to influence your business in a negative way. You should find your purpose and stay grounded.

Finally, entrepreneurs should have interpersonal skills. They must have the ability to establish and maintain positive relationships with customers and clients, employees, financial lenders, and investors, among others. An entrepreneur does not have to be the smartest or highly achieved person, but he or she needs to build a team that can work together. A good team can lead to more success in the business and can be more beneficial than working alone. It is very important to keep your team motivated.

What to Remember

1. Make sure that what you are working on, is something you really like to do. Entrepreneurship entails so much hard work and it is very critical to ensure that you are following the right path. Amini said. "If this is something you really want, then think long-term and be persistent". "The vast majority of great entrepreneurs failed multiple times before they finally found the business idea that took off and brought them success."

2. Learn from your failures and the failures of others. It is very necessary to study the businesses that end up failing, rather than admiring the small percentage of businesses that grow to become successful. This research will greatly increase your chances of success, since most companies have made common mistakes that have led

to their downfall. Paving your way to success is actually having the humility to learn from the mistakes of others before making them yourself.

3. Focus on solving problems. Entrepreneurs should always be in search of problems to solve and not the other way around. Although we have cases where entrepreneurs create something and then start looking for a problem to fit in their innovation, trying to solve a problem with your innovation carries more weight and problem-solving is always more useful. This may not always be the case in the short-run; however, it will definitely apply more frequently on a long-term basis.

4. Get advice from those who have done similar things. It is appropriate for business owners to find mentors who are successful, as well as to read books, network with people they admire, and look into great educational programs to help them throughout the process. Baby steps count. Seize the opportunity you have and use it wisely. You should not wait for luck because it will easily pass you by. Even though getting advice from others is very helpful, you have to believe in yourself. Your instincts and intuition are also very helpful and will lead you to where you are supposed to be.

5. Be passionate about what you do. To be successful, you should find your passion and then build a business around it. Gottlieb said, "The passion is what will get you through the stumbling

blocks and prevent you from quitting in the middle of the race."
Follow your passion and do something that you are totally committed to do. You need to have a vision, not only charisma. That is:

➢ Having in mind what you are about to do – Vision
➢ Coordinate the vision into a tangible substance – Sense-making capability
➢ Connect the substance with issues that can turn it into reality - Relationship to make things happen
➢ Use the relationship you have along with tools to build your vision - Technology
➢ Overcome all the obstacles and build your own business - Executing skills, making it happen

<u>Creative thinking</u>

1. What are some common obstacles of entrepreneurship?
2. How does a creative mind build and maintain vision?
3. Create an imaginary company while analysing the skills and materials you need.

Financing your Project

In order to turn your business idea into an incredible success or to take your existing business to the next level of growth, you will need capital to invest in it. There are a number of funds and incentives available to support your business venture, and turn your entrepreneurial dreams into a reality. Most often the application process is complex and confusing. One has to determine which grant he or she is qualified for, which incentives would benefit his or her company the most, and how to get started.

There are many organizations worldwide that support entrepreneurs. They have different criteria, depending on the project you want to involve yourself in. Below are some ways to get support for your business. If you are able to present a project very well, creating a good business plan, then the chance of getting support is high. The use of the Internet is widespread, and this is a very useful tool to get more information and to help finance your business.

A very good way to get support, especially when you are living in a less developed country, is to borrow from family and friends. They are a frequent source of funding for small businesses. In order to maintain your family and friendly relationship, make sure that you have a good business plan and have done enough research that the business you are trying to do is going to earn you capital with interest. That way, you will be able to pay back the money you borrow.

There are also **angel capital groups**, which support businesses that have good potential to grow to a significant size. These are investors who are out to make money. So you have to make a business plan, and be able to prove that you have the experience to run the business and that the business will make enough money and profit for them as investors. There are a number of organizations that are focused on providing funding for business ventures that can make a difference to the economy. These include organizations such as the Department of Trade and Industry (DTI), National Empowerment Fund (NEF), National Youth Development Agency (NYDA) in South Africa, and African Development Foundation (ADF) found in Benin, Botswana, Cape Verde, Ghana, Guinea, Mali, Namibia, Niger, Nigeria, Senegal, Swaziland, Tanzania, Uganda, Zambia, and Zimbabwe. There are many other funding organizations that focus on different aspects in economic development. A list of some of them can be found at the end of the book.

You can also apply for a business loan or a micro loan. In the case of micro loans, capital is available through a variety of resources including online lenders, community sources, and peer lending groups.

This means the size of the loan, eligibility, interest rates and terms vary according to the source. Unlike a business loan, you are dealing with a bank. You will need to give the bank information like the purpose of the loan, the amount of investment in the business by the owner(s), the projected opening-day balance sheet (new businesses), the projections of income, expenses and cash flow, any lease details, signed personal financial statements, and your resume or curriculum vitae. You may also need a formal business plan. Do not be surprised if the bank turns you down. They are out to make gains and ensure they get their money back. That is why they are very strict on the information provided.

Using a credit card is also a good way to get money to start a business. But in most developing countries, very few are in possession of credit cards, and these cards have limits. So there is a possibility to get instant credit by using the card up to the limit. Equipment, suppliers, and other small items can be purchased with a credit card. But using a credit card to start your business bears some significant risk as well. You can easily run up a huge credit card bill, which you will be responsible for paying, whether your business is successful or not.

An important aspect that we should not neglect is **Crowdfunding**. There are many successful businesses today that started through crowdfunding. Crowdfunding sites make it possible to raise small amounts of money from a lot of people. You have to present your project on the crowdfunding sites and if the project is interesting for the people, they will support you. But remember that crowdfunding makes the idea of your business product or service public. That means if you need to keep your idea confidential, do not use Crowdfunding. Some Crowdfunding platforms are: JumpStart Africa, RealtyAfrica, Thundafund, Lelapa Fund, Usizo, etc.

You can fund your business by applying for a home equity or property line of credit. Some banks offer home equity lines of credit that let you borrow up to as much as 75% of the appraised value of your home. Your private assets are being considered as well to ensure that the loan is paid. The amount of money you get depends on the value of your home and the other properties you own. So you should really be intent on succeeding because any failure will lead to the loss of your home and anything associated to the loan.

How to manage your capital

In order to be successful in business, you should know how to save money and reinvest it wisely. You can save money by reducing the cost of your daily activities. For example, you could drink water instead of buying soft drinks or beer, you could reduce your electricity consumption through switching off the television instead of letting it run the whole day, and you could shop at bargain outlets instead of purchasing expensive clothes, etc. There are, of course, many ways to minimise cost. In case you have a savings account, use some of the money for the start up. But do not use all of the money. You will need to have some reserve in case of emergencies.

Start your business from home. If you do not have enough capital, you can start your business for much less money at home. You do not have to foot the bill for office space and utilities for an out-of-the-home office. You may not want to advertise that you are working from home, but you can save a lot of money by doing this.

Start your business on a part time basis and get a part time job. The part time job will provide you with a steady source of income. If you are already working, do not quit your job. You can work to earn enough money to start your business, and use that steady income to supplement the income of your new business until it is producing enough for you to phase out the additional work.

Rent or buy used equipment. There are some items that your business does not need on a regular basis. Also, you may not be very sure how much you will need to use certain items. There are shops that rent business items instead of you having to buy them, so you can try them out before committing to them on a permanent basis. Through this method you can save a lot of capital. After knowing exactly what you need, especially on a regular basis, you could then purchase the item as used instead of new. You should only think of replacing these items when you have gathered enough capital. Search the web or ask your friends, colleagues and family members for items such as "used restaurant equipment", "used market benches" or "used office furniture" etc.

Business Plan

A business plan is a working document which includes all the goals and strategies of a company with the basic requirements, projects and actions for a specific time frame. A business plan has several tasks to fulfil. It is used outside the company to convince potential funders and it is used within the company to build a basis for further strategy and planning concepts. The plan should be well structured and carry the important points of your business. The business plan portrays your business idea and how you are going to generate income and make profit out of your business. This chapter highlights the main points of a business plan and its content. These are actually guidelines and should therefore be adjusted depending on what business idea you have and are about to implement.

The first topic on your business plan should be your business idea. You have to define this very concretely. It does not mean that you have to explain every detail of the business, but the explanation should be clear in a way that if a third person reads it, he will be able to know exactly what the business is about and the main idea on how to generate income from the business idea. Try to avoid complicated words. The writing should suit your target audience as well. You can also use graphics and pictures, if necessary. The whole description should not be more than two to three pages depending on how complicated your business idea is. You should be able to answer questions like:

- What is the main item or subject of the Company?
- When do you want to start?
- What are your products and services?
- How will you generate capital from the business?
- Which audience are you targeting?

It is very necessary to start with the general information and then break it down into some detail. This general information enables you to categorize your product.

The second important topic on your business plan is the place of your market operation. If you already have a place where you are operating, you can take pictures of it and add it to your plan. Explain why this area is the best for your business. You should not write more than one or two pages. The following questions can help you when writing:

- How is your business location constructed?
- How big is it?
- What are the characteristics of the location?
- What are the special details that are important to be known?
- How much will it cost you a month?
- Why is the location the best place to start your business?

It is also necessary to point out the disadvantages of the location, if there are any. But then you have to explain how you are going to compensate for these disadvantages. Make sure that the pictures you use give a positive effect for your location.

The next topic is your audience and the area in which you want to operate. You should be able to describe the area in which you are planning to do business and the target group in it. You can define these using socio-demographic criteria like age, sex, profession and income, if you are dealing directly with consumers (for example, in private households). If you want to deal with other companies, then you should identify criteria like the area and size of the company. You should be able to describe the strategy or the marketing plan you will use to convince your target group to go for your product or services. One to two pages will be enough for this discussion. Questions you should ask include:

- Which region are you interested in?
- How many citizens/companies are there?
- What are their age groups?
- What are the attributes that can be associated to your target group?
- How have you allocated your offer to meet the requirements of your target group?

If you are not very sure how to define your target group, you can take an example of a competitive company and conduct an interview with their customers.

Our next topic is the market analysis. You have to determine the market in which your target group is found. This is very difficult if you are just starting your business or if it is a completely new innovation where there are no statistics. You can easily find statistics online or in some institutions, councils and reports from the different company branches. Use only updated statistics. These should not be older than three years in order to obtain a real picture of your business. You should write down about two pages and here are some questions to help you complete this chapter:

- What actually is my market?
- How do I define my market?
- How big is the market?
- How have other companies in my area developed in the past three to five years?

With this information, you will have a better overview of your business and how it will possibly develop. It is always necessary to write down the source of your information. If you can find one, ask a professional in the area or you can also conduct interviews to get the necessary information you need.

Our next topic is competition analysis. Here you have to analyse who the competitors are in your potential market. It is necessary to consider not only the companies that offer the same product that you do, but also companies that offer similar products or substitutes and services. You will need about one to two pages for this chapter. Important questions include:

- Who are the competitors?
- Where are they located?
- How have they positioned themselves?
- How do you want to stand out from them?

-   What is your unique feature?

Always remain objective in your description and bring out facts. You can make a test by buying or using a competitor's services. By doing so, you will be able to evaluate both the advantages and disadvantages of the competitor.

Our next point focuses on the marketing plan. You have to describe how you will convince your target group to purchase your goods or services. Since this is a very important point, especially with start-ups, you have to really focus on it and develop a good marketing strategy. You will need about two to three pages for this. Questions to be asked include:

-   What can I do to reach almost all of my target group?
-   What is the composition of my marketing plan and advertise-ment?
-   How much money do I want to invest in marketing?
-   How does the company present itself?
-   Is there already existing contact with potential customers?

If you already have a logo of the company, you can show it on your marketing plan. What you have to avoid is to name numerous possible marking activities that you could do. Stay short and precise. Set a specific goal and try to reach it. You have to concretise which strategy you will use for the beginning and which advertising strategy you will use regularly.

Our next topic focuses on the price. You have to determine the price category of your goods and services. You do not need to display your complete product-price catalogue, but you should pick out some of the main products and display them with their prices. This should cover about two pages. The following questions will help you in your writing:

- Which goods and services are offered and at what price?
- How do you calculate the price?
- Are your prices higher or lower than that of your competitors?

When calculating the price, it is good to use the net prices and any tax increase could be added to it. This is to make sure that you do not make the price extremely low. Go for average prices. You can get this by comparing prices of your competitors.

The next topic is planning the company's manpower. The quality of your workers determines the company's growth. The most important part here is to get good workers, and secondly to motivate them to work with you in the long run. So you have to discuss in this chapter the strategy you will use to acquire new workers and what criteria you will use to pick out the best workers for yourself. The number of pages should be about two. Some central questions are:

- How many workers do you want to employ?
- How are you going to get these workers?
- Which characteristics and traits should they have?
- How much will they earn?
- How do you want to motivate them in the long run?

If you already have somebody who is willing to work with you, you can mention it in the business plan and even add his or her Curriculum Vitae to it.

The next point is describing the kind of business person or entrepreneur you are. You have to prove that you are able to run the company. You should focus on your know how of the product as well as your management and educational capacity. This should be about one to two pages and you should consider these central questions:

- What experience do you have in this area?
- What are the requirements you need?
- What is your level of education and which additional seminars do you have?
- What are your soft and strong skills as an entrepreneur?

When describing all of this, it is necessary to explain everything in relation to your business idea. All the necessary certificates and documents you have should be added to the business plan.

The tenth point is the SWOT-Analysis (Fig. 5). You have to describe your Strengths, Weaknesses, Opportunities and Threats. Your focus should be more on your strengths and opportunities rather than your weaknesses and threats. Make sure that you are able to compensate for your weaknesses and threats. Bring out examples of worst case issues and how you resolved the problem. This should take about two pages and you should think of questions like:

- What are my strengths?
- What are my weaknesses?
- What are the opportunities you have?
- What are the threats?
- How do I compensate for my threats and weaknesses?

You should avoid using standard forms or answers but try to answer the questions in a way that actually suits your business plan. You can discuss the analysis with a friend or family member. At least, they will have a critical view of it.

Fig. 5

SWOT Analysis[v]

	Opportunities *External, positive*	Threats *External, negative*
Strengths *Internal, positive*	How do you use your strengths to maximise your opportunities	How do you use your strengths to minimise your threats
Weaknesses *Internal, negative*	How do you ensure that weaknesses will not stop you from opportunities	How will you fix weaknesses that can make threats have a real impact

The next topic is to plan your investment. Here you have to describe your investment at the beginning of the project and other main investments that will follow up later on. These amount should be added together in order to determine the sum of the investment. The sum is the amount of capital you need to start your business. It is important to be concrete and specific in the amount you provide. The best way is to look for quotes which you can attach to the business plan. This can have about three to four pages. Questions to ask are:

- How much do I need for my goods and services?
- How much do I need for machines?
- What are my fixed costs?
- What are the variable costs?
- Do you need some capital for a one-time investment in the future?

You should also consider the investment already in use. That is, if you are using your house or machine for your start-up, then you should also consider this in the business plan using the actual market value. You should not forget to add any form of related taxes that may be applicable.

Our next point is planning the operating costs. You have to describe how you determined the prices. You can do this by requesting quotes before writing your business plan. You should also attach these quotes to the business plan. In cases where you cannot ask for a quote, it is a good idea to consult an expert in the area. Operational costs are for instance, personal costs, occupancy costs, advertisement costs, depreciation allowances and other costs. There are a lot of operational costs, which you really have to analyse very well. You will need about for pages for this. Some general questions are:

- What are the costs that will allow me to function as a company?
- Do I have the quotes for my purchases?
- Are the costs appropriate?

Creating a table can help you have a better view of the operational costs. You could create two tables, one showing the actual costs and the other giving a prediction of the costs for the next three years.

The next point is planning the total revenue of the business. This is actually an estimated value. It is difficult to determine this value with a start-up firm since there are no past values on which you can depend. Nevertheless, you can concentrate on the market value of your area or use the statistics of your competitors. Consider the advertisements, the regional pricing and the average revenue in this area. Since this is one of the most important topics of the business plan, you have to be very precise in what you are doing. If you do not have expertise in calculations, it would be wise to look for professional help.

Our next topic is the cost-effectiveness plan. The goal here is to produce an efficient revenue plan. You will have to deduct the production cost from the revenue, and from this you will get the earnings. From these earnings you will need to deduct the operational costs; you will then have the end sum without tax. Most companies, especially start-ups, always plan for a loss during the first year. This is also very possible since you are still new in the market and not well known. But you have to develop fast and change the minus records into a positive balance sheet. This page has to cover about two pages.

Our last point is cash flow. Here it is important to know the amount of cash budget you have on hand and not in a period. The outgoing payment will be deducted from the incoming payment. The cash flow can be your own capital (net equity) or a credit. The cash flow should be noted on a monthly basis, and you have to provide this information for at least three months on your business plan. Since it is very broad, it could take about six pages.

There are, of course, other aspects that you can consider when creating a business plan that are not mentioned here. It actually depends on the scope of the business you are trying to undertake.

Creative Thinking

1. How do you conserve food that will last for at least three months?
2. Set up a business plan for a food conservation company.
3. Create a financial plan for your food company.

Sample Formal Business Plan Outline

1.0 Business Idea/Executive Summary

1.1 Problem

1.2 Solution

1.3 Target Audience/Market

1.4 Competition

2.0 Products and Services

2.1 Validation of Problem and Solution

2.2 Roadmap/Future Plans

3.0 Market Analysis Summary

3.1 Market Needs

3.2 Market Trends

3.3 Market Growth

3.4 Key Customers

6.0 Financial Plan

6.1 Revenue/Sales Forecast

6.2 Expenses

6.3 Projected Profit and Loss

6.4 Projected Cash Flow

6.5 Projected Balance Sheet

Conclusion

Innovation and creativity help to develop a country and promote growth. There is a lot of cash flow from Africans in the diaspora into the different African countries. On the one hand, this capital helps to save lives and educate children, but on the other hand, it retards economic growth. That is why educating the children now to have an entrepreneurial mind set will promote a stable economic growth in the long-run. Building up your own business is not a very easy task, but having the right passion and commitment to it usually leads to success. The government should create an atmosphere that favours and promotes entrepreneurship by promoting investment and discouraging migration. When we start thinking in the right direction, we react in a cautious way.

In many underdeveloped countries, the citizens migrate to other areas to improve their standards of living. These migrants work really hard to secure a better living for themselves and their families. In order to get a good source of income in a foreign land, you should have a real perspective and a good educational background. Unfortunately, most African migrants do not have this and therefore rarely have a good source of income and become slaves to work. Therefore it is terribly important to teach African children now to be aware of their environment and to learn how to build their own business. They have to develop courage to face the challenges of entrepreneurship, for at that age the mind is active and it is ready to reach out for new ideas. One just has to create space for those new ideas. These children can learn to be good leaders of tomorrow, be creative and tell their own stories. They will learn from the entrepreneurs of today. The entrepreneurial journey starts with you, and nobody can tell your story better than you.

Appendices

Appendix A: References

Henry, C., Hill, F. and Leitch, C. (2003). Entrepreneurship Education and Training: the Issue of Effectiveness. England: Ashgate.

Hisrich R. & Peters M. (2011), Entrepreneurship, 8th Edition. McGraw Hill Publishers.

Janet Attard, (2000), Business Know-How small business web site and information resource: An Operational Guide For Home-Based and Micro-Sized Businesses with Limited Budgets, Adams Media Corporation

Janet Attard, (n.d.), Where to Get Money to Start a Business, Retrieved from http://www.businessknowhow.com/money/startup-money.htm

Nabi, G., Holden, R. and Walmsley, A. (2006). Graduate career-making and business start-up: A literature review. Education & Training, 48, 373-385.

Ng, F. & Yeats, AJ. (2000). On the recent trade performance of Sub-Saharan African countries: Cause for hope or more of the same? (African Region Working Papers Series, #7). Washington, DC: The World Bank.

Paula Fernandes, (2016, March 21), What is Entrepreneurship?, Retrieved from http://www.businessnewsdaily.com/2642entrepreneur ship.html#sthash.vGDrB1xK.dpuf

Rathgeber, E. M., & Adera, E. O. (Eds.). (2000). Gender and the information revolution in Africa. Ottawa: International Development Research Center (IDRC).

Svensson, J. (2000). The cost of doing business: Firms' experience with corruption in Uganda. (African Region Working Paper Series, #6). Washington, D.C.: The World Bank.

Tim Strawson and Cordelia Lonsdale, Improving ODA allocation for a post 2015 world (2014-2015) Retrieved from http://www.un.org/en/ ecosoc/newfunct/pdf15/un_improving_oda_allocation_for_post-2015_world.pdf

Businessplan – Bauplan zum erfolgreichen Unternehmen, (n.d.), Retrieved from http://www.businessplan.org

Gross Domestic Product (GDP), (n.d.), Business Dictionary, Retrieved from http://www.businessdictionary.com/definition/gross-domestic-product GDP.html#ixzz41V27VeyG

Investopedia Staff, (2015, march 26), What is GDP and why is it so important to economists and investors?, Retrieved from http://www.investopedia.com/ask/answers/199.asp#ixzz41UzoVU1m

Organisations Grants for Africa, (2016, March 20), Retrieved from http://www.advance-africa.com/Grants-for-NGOs-and Organisations.html

Regional distribution of global population by region, 2010 and 2050 (2013), Retrieved from http://www.pewresearch.org

Resources for Importing from & Exporting to Africa (2016, March 21), Retrieved from http://www.afrst.illinois.edu/outreach/business /imports/%23E

Definitions and Glossary terms, Retrieved from

http://www.dictionary.com, (August 2016)

http://www.businessdictionary.com (August 2016)

https://en.wikipedia.org (August 2016)

Appendix B: Funding Agencies

African Development Foundation Grants

African Doctoral Dissertation Research Fellowship

Africa Foundation Grants

Africa Grantmakers' Affinity Group -AGAG

Africa Organizations Grants

Africa Small Grants

African Women Development Fund

African Women in Agricultural R & D - (AWARD)

Aga Khan Development Network - AKDN

AGFUND International Prize

Agricultural Development Grants

Allan & Nesta Ferguson Charitable Trust Grants

Allen Foundation Inc. Grants

Alliance of Civilizations Youth Solidarity Fund

Ark Foundation of Africa - AFA

Ashden Awards for Sustainable Energy

Autobloggreen Grant

Award for Human Rights Defenders

Awards Creative Women and Women's Groups

Baxter International Foundation Grants

BBC World Challenge Competition

Bernard van Leer Foundation

Borlaug Award for Field Research

Building Capacity Fellowships

Call for Proposals in Good Governance & Human Rights

Canadian Executive Service Organization

Captain Planet Foundation Grants

Children's Investment Fund Foundation Grants - CIFF

Clinical Research Course

Coca-Cola Foundation Grants

Common Fund for Commodities Grants

Commonwealth Foundation's Civil Society Responsive Grants

Commonwealth Youth Awards

Conference or Training Grant- Kirkhouse Trust

Conservation Food and Health Foundation Grants

Dell Social Innovation Competition

EABL Foundation Grants (Grants for NGOs and Organisations)

Educating Africa Pan-African Awards for Entrepreneurship in Education

Elizabeth Neuffer Fellowship

Fahamu Pan-African Fellowship (FPAF) Program

Family Care Foundation Grants (FCF)

Feed the Children Grants

Feed the Minds Grants

Funding and Grants for NGOs

Funds to Help End Violence Against Women

Gates Vaccine Innovation Award

GEF Small Grants

Gen Foundation Grants

Gender and Agriculture/Rural Development Grants

Geotourism Challenge Award

Glimmer of Hope Foundation - Ethiopia

Global Development Awards and Medals Competition

Global Fund for Community Foundations

Global Fund for Children (GFC) Grants

Global Fund for Women Grants

Grant Competition for Peacebuilding Projects

Grants for Buea Conference on Mathematical Sciences

Grants for Health Projects

Grants for Innovative Libraries

HelpAge International (Grants for NGOs and Organisations)

Hewlett-Packard (HP) Philanthropy

HIV/AIDS Treatment And Prevention Programs Grants

HP EdTech Innovators Award

Human Rights Prize

Human Rights Small Grants Scheme

Humanitarian Innovation Grants

IDRC and DFID Call for Concept Notes on Climate Change Adaptation

International Grant Competition

International Women's Programs Grants

International Youth Foundation Grants

Joseph Rowntree Charitable Trust

Koch Foundation Grants

Loyola Foundation Grants

Mama Cash Grants

McKnight Foundation Grants

Monsanto Fund Grants

NGOs in Kenya Funding & Grants

NGOs Small Grants Programme

Nippon Foundation Grants

Oak Foundation Grants

ONE Africa Award

Opportunity Grants for US Education

Peace Stone Foundation Grants

Progressive Educational Fund (PEF)

Project Development Grants

Project Grant - Aid to the Church in Need

Red Umbrella Fund

Requests for Proposals in Nutrition

Rufford Small Grant For Nature Conservation

Sasakawa Peace Foundation Grants for NGOs

Saving Lives at Birth Grants

Scholar Grants

SeaWorld Grants for Organizations and Individuals

SIDA Call for Proposals

Sightsavers Innovation Fund

Skoll Awards for Social Entrepreneurship

Small Grants for Women

Social Innovation in Health Initiative

STARS Impact Awards for NGOs

Staying Alive Foundation Awards

Stephen Lewis Foundation support for HIV/AIDS

SURVIVE-MIVA Grants for the Developing World

Swiss Re International ReSource Award

The Christensen Fund Grants

The Disability Rights Fund

The Lourdes Arizpe Award - Grants for NGOs and Organisations

The Monsanto Fund Grants - Grants for NGOs and Organisations

The Nestle Prize

The Ramsar Convention Small Grants Fund

The United Nations Public Service Awards - Grants for NGOs and Organisations

Think Tank Initiative Funding for NGOs

Tony Elumelu Foundation Entrepreneurship Programme

TWAS-AAS-Microsoft Award for Young Scientists

TWAS Grants for Scientific Meetings in Developing Countries

UN-HABITAT Youth Fund for NGOs and CBOs

UNEP Sasakawa Prize

UNESCO/ANSTI Diaspora Award

UNESCO-Aschberg Bursaries

UNFPA Special Youth Programme Grants

UN.GIFT Small Grants

UNHCR Nansen Refugee Award

United Nations Democracy Fund (UNDEF) Grants

United Nations Population Award

UN Permanent Forum Grants

USAID Development Grants Program

Appendix C: Glossary of Terms

African Growth and Opportunity Act (AGOA)

An Act to authorize a new trade and investment policy for sub-Saharan Africa. The purpose of this legislation is to assist the economies of sub-Saharan Africa and to improve economic relations between the United States and the region. After completing its initial 15-year period of validity, the AGOA legislation was extended on 29 June 2015 by a further 10 years, to 2025

Angel Capital Group

It is a group of affluent individual who provides capital for a business start-up, usually in exchange for convertible debt or ownership equity.

Bottom-Up

A movement of an activity or an entity that begins at a low level and proceeds to progress upwards.

Business Plan

It is a detailed plan setting out the objectives of a business, the strategy and tactics planned to achieve them, and the expected profits, usually over a period of three to ten years

Capitalism

An economic system in which investment in and ownership of the means of production, distribution, and exchange of wealth is made and maintained chiefly by private individuals or corporations, especially as contrasted to cooperatively or state-owned means of wealth.

Cash flow

The sum of the after-tax profit of a business plus depreciation and other noncash charges: used as an indication of internal funds available for stock dividends, purchase of buildings and equipment, etc.

Corrupt

An act of dishonest practices, as bribery; lacking integrity; crooked.

Crowdfunding

The method of raising money from a large amount of individual investors, typically through the Internet, for a project or organization.

Education

The act or process of imparting or acquiring general knowledge, developing the powers of reasoning and judgment, and generally of preparing oneself or others intellectually for mature life.

Entrepreneur

An entrepreneur is a person who organizes and manages any enterprise, especially a business, usually with considerable initiative and risk. **Entrepreneurship** is the capacity and willingness to develop, organize and manage a business venture along with any of its risks in order to make a profit.

Gross domestic product (GDP)

It is a monetary measure of the market value of all final goods and services produced in a period (quarterly or yearly). Nominal GDP estimates are commonly used to determine the economic performance of a whole country or region, and to make international comparisons. Nominal GDP, however, does not reflect differences in the cost of living and the inflation rates of the countries. Real GDP measures the value of economic output adjusted for price changes (i.e., inflation or deflation)

- **Output Approach**

  The sum of the gross values added of all resident, institutional units engaged in production (plus any taxes, and minus any subsidies, on products not included in the value of their outputs)

- **Income Approach**

  The sum of primary incomes distributed by resident producer units.

- **Expenditure Approach**

  the sum of the final uses of goods and services (all uses except intermediate consumption) measured in purchasers' prices.

Imperfect Information

Information that only reduces uncertainty but (unlike perfect information) does not eliminate it.

Inclusion (inclusive capitalism)

Inclusion is when every citizen receives the value and outcome of growth

Innovation

The process of translating an idea or invention into a good or service that creates value or for which customers will pay.

Investors

A person who put (money) to use, by purchase or expenditure, in something offering potential profitable returns, as interest, income, or appreciation in value.

Leadership

The position or function of a leader, a person who guides or directs a group.

Marketing

The total of activities involved in the transfer of goods from the producer or seller to the consumer or buyer, including advertising, shipping, storing, and selling.

Micro and Macro levels

Micro-level focuses on individuals and their interactions meanwhile macro-level focuses more upon social structure, social processes and problems, and their interrelationships

Official development assistance (ODA)

It is a term coined by the Development Assistance Committee (DAC) of the Organisation for Economic Co-operation and Development (OECD) to measure aid.

Perfect information

Information that completely eliminates uncertainty in a situation, as opposed to imperfect information which only reduces uncertainty.

Production

The creation of value; the producing of articles having exchange value

Top-Down

An approach in decision making in which the desired results or objectives of a decided upon first and then methods to achieve them are selected.

Appendix D: Table of Figures

---

[i] Source: AFDB, OECD, UNDP, African economic Outlook 2014

[ii] Euromonitor International from national statis-

tics/Eurostat/OECD/UN/IMF

[iii] Major Export commodities and originating countries

[iv] Regional distribution of global population by region, 2010 and 2050
(2013) Retrieved from http://www.pewresearch.org on August 15, 2016.

[v] SWOT Analysis

Zeitfracht Medien GmbH
Ferdinand-Jühlke-Straße 7
99095 Erfurt, Deutschland
produktsicherheit@kolibri360.de